50 Gut-Friendly Dish Recipes for Home

By: Kelly Johnson

Table of Contents

- Classic Beef Stew
- Chicken Alfredo Pasta
- Vegetable Stir-Fry with Rice
- BBQ Ribs
- Spaghetti Bolognese
- Turkey and Cheese Sandwich
- Beef Burritos
- Grilled Salmon with Vegetables
- Chili Cheese Hot Dogs
- Tuna Salad Wrap
- Pork Chops with Mashed Potatoes
- Veggie Burger
- Teriyaki Chicken Skewers
- Shrimp Fried Rice
- Beef Tacos
- Chicken Caesar Salad
- Meatball Subs
- Greek Gyros
- Macaroni and Cheese
- Hawaiian Pizza
- BLT Sandwich
- Beef and Broccoli Stir-Fry
- Italian Sausage Penne
- Egg Salad Wrap
- Chicken Quesadillas
- Sloppy Joes
- Asian Noodle Salad
- Vegetable Soup
- Pulled BBQ Chicken Sandwich
- Buffalo Chicken Wings
- Beef Kebabs
- Fish Tacos
- Pesto Pasta with Grilled Chicken
- Ham and Cheese Panini
- Beef and Bean Burritos

- Caesar Salad with Grilled Shrimp
- Veggie Stir-Fried Rice
- Chicken Enchiladas
- Pepperoni Pizza
- Corned Beef Hash
- Spinach and Feta Stuffed Chicken
- Bacon, Lettuce, and Tomato Wrap
- Teriyaki Beef Bowl
- Chicken Fajitas
- Italian Sub Sandwich
- Veggie and Hummus Wrap
- Beef Stroganoff
- Baked Lemon Herb Cod
- Pulled Pork Sliders
- Thai Peanut Noodles

Classic Beef Stew

Ingredients:

- 2 lbs stewing beef, cut into cubes
- 2 tablespoons vegetable oil
- 4 cups beef broth
- 1 onion, chopped
- 3 cloves garlic, minced
- 4 carrots, peeled and sliced
- 3 potatoes, peeled and diced
- 1 cup frozen peas
- 2 tablespoons tomato paste
- 1 tablespoon Worcestershire sauce
- 1 teaspoon dried thyme
- Salt and pepper, to taste

Instructions:

1. Heat the vegetable oil in a large pot or Dutch oven over medium-high heat.
2. Add the beef cubes in batches and brown them on all sides. Remove and set aside.
3. In the same pot, add the chopped onion and minced garlic. Sauté until softened.
4. Return the browned beef to the pot. Add beef broth, tomato paste, Worcestershire sauce, and dried thyme. Stir to combine.
5. Bring the mixture to a boil, then reduce the heat to low. Cover and simmer for about 1.5 to 2 hours, or until the beef is tender.
6. Add the sliced carrots and diced potatoes to the pot. Continue to simmer, covered, for another 30 minutes or until the vegetables are tender.
7. Stir in the frozen peas and cook for an additional 5 minutes.
8. Season with salt and pepper to taste.
9. Serve hot, optionally garnished with fresh chopped parsley.

Enjoy your classic beef stew, a hearty and comforting meal perfect for any occasion!

Chicken Alfredo Pasta

Ingredients:

- 8 oz fettuccine pasta
- 2 boneless, skinless chicken breasts, cut into strips
- 2 tablespoons butter
- 2 cloves garlic, minced
- 1 cup heavy cream
- 1 cup grated Parmesan cheese
- Salt and pepper, to taste
- Chopped fresh parsley, for garnish (optional)

Instructions:

1. Cook the fettuccine pasta according to package instructions. Drain and set aside.
2. In a large skillet, melt the butter over medium-high heat.
3. Add the chicken breast strips to the skillet and cook until golden brown and cooked through, about 5-7 minutes per side. Remove the cooked chicken from the skillet and set aside.
4. In the same skillet, add minced garlic and cook for about 30 seconds until fragrant.
5. Reduce the heat to medium-low. Pour in the heavy cream, stirring constantly until heated through.
6. Gradually add the grated Parmesan cheese to the skillet, stirring continuously until the cheese is melted and the sauce is smooth and creamy.
7. Season the Alfredo sauce with salt and pepper to taste.
8. Add the cooked fettuccine pasta to the skillet, tossing well to coat the pasta evenly with the sauce.
9. Return the cooked chicken strips to the skillet, mixing with the pasta and Alfredo sauce.
10. Cook for an additional 2-3 minutes until everything is heated through.
11. Garnish with chopped fresh parsley if desired.
12. Serve hot and enjoy your creamy Chicken Alfredo Pasta!

This Chicken Alfredo Pasta is a delicious and satisfying dish that is perfect for a comforting meal at home or on the road. Adjust the seasoning and thickness of the sauce according to your preference.

Vegetable Stir-Fry with Rice

Ingredients:

- 1 cup uncooked white or brown rice
- 2 tablespoons vegetable oil
- 2 cups mixed vegetables (such as bell peppers, broccoli, carrots, snow peas, mushrooms)
- 1 onion, thinly sliced
- 3 cloves garlic, minced
- 1-inch piece of ginger, minced
- 1/4 cup soy sauce
- 1 tablespoon oyster sauce (optional)
- 1 tablespoon hoisin sauce (optional)
- Salt and pepper, to taste
- Sliced green onions, for garnish (optional)
- Sesame seeds, for garnish (optional)

Instructions:

1. Cook the rice according to package instructions. Set aside.
2. In a large skillet or wok, heat the vegetable oil over medium-high heat.
3. Add the sliced onion, minced garlic, and minced ginger to the skillet. Stir-fry for 1-2 minutes until fragrant.
4. Add the mixed vegetables to the skillet. Stir-fry for 3-4 minutes until they start to soften but are still crisp.
5. In a small bowl, whisk together the soy sauce, oyster sauce (if using), and hoisin sauce (if using).
6. Pour the sauce mixture over the vegetables in the skillet. Stir well to coat all the vegetables evenly.
7. Continue to stir-fry for another 1-2 minutes until the vegetables are cooked to your desired tenderness.
8. Season with salt and pepper to taste.
9. Add the cooked rice to the skillet, tossing well with the vegetables and sauce.
10. Cook for an additional 1-2 minutes to heat everything through.
11. Remove from heat and garnish with sliced green onions and sesame seeds if desired.
12. Serve hot as a delicious and nutritious Vegetable Stir-Fry with Rice!

This vegetable stir-fry is a versatile and healthy dish that can be customized with your favorite vegetables and sauces. It's quick and easy to prepare, making it perfect for a satisfying meal on the road or at home. Adjust the seasoning and sauce quantities according to your taste preferences. Enjoy!

BBQ Ribs

Ingredients:

- 2 racks of pork baby back ribs (about 4-5 pounds total)
- Salt and black pepper, to taste
- BBQ rub or seasoning blend
- 1 cup BBQ sauce (store-bought or homemade)

Instructions:

1. Preheat your grill or oven to 300°F (150°C).
2. If using the oven, line a baking sheet with foil for easy cleanup.
3. Remove the membrane from the back of the ribs: Slide a knife under the membrane to loosen, then grab it with a paper towel and pull it off.
4. Season the ribs generously with salt, black pepper, and your favorite BBQ rub or seasoning blend. Make sure to coat both sides of the ribs.
5. Place the ribs on the grill or in the oven. If grilling, place them bone-side down over indirect heat.
6. Cook the ribs low and slow: Grill or bake for about 2.5-3 hours, or until the ribs are tender and the meat starts to pull away from the bones.
7. During the last 30 minutes of cooking, baste the ribs with BBQ sauce, brushing it on both sides. Continue cooking until the sauce is sticky and caramelized.
8. Remove the ribs from the grill or oven and let them rest for a few minutes.
9. Cut the ribs between the bones into individual pieces.
10. Serve hot with extra BBQ sauce on the side, if desired.

Enjoy these tender and flavorful BBQ ribs, a classic favorite that's perfect for a hearty meal on the road or at home. Adjust the cooking time based on the thickness of your ribs and your desired level of tenderness.

Spaghetti Bolognese

Ingredients:

- 8 oz spaghetti
- 1 tablespoon olive oil
- 1 onion, finely chopped
- 2 cloves garlic, minced
- 1 carrot, finely diced
- 1 celery stalk, finely diced
- 1 lb ground beef (or a combination of beef and pork)
- 1 can (14 oz) crushed tomatoes
- 2 tablespoons tomato paste
- 1/2 cup beef or chicken broth
- 1/2 cup red wine (optional)
- 1 teaspoon dried oregano
- 1 teaspoon dried basil
- Salt and pepper, to taste
- Grated Parmesan cheese, for serving
- Chopped fresh parsley, for garnish (optional)

Instructions:

1. Cook the spaghetti according to package instructions. Drain and set aside.
2. In a large skillet or pot, heat the olive oil over medium heat.
3. Add the chopped onion, minced garlic, diced carrot, and diced celery to the skillet. Cook for 5-6 minutes, or until the vegetables are softened.
4. Add the ground beef to the skillet. Cook, breaking it up with a spoon, until browned and cooked through.
5. Stir in the crushed tomatoes, tomato paste, beef or chicken broth, and red wine (if using).
6. Season with dried oregano, dried basil, salt, and pepper. Stir well to combine.
7. Bring the sauce to a simmer. Reduce the heat to low, cover, and let it simmer gently for 30-40 minutes, stirring occasionally.
8. Taste and adjust seasoning if needed.
9. Serve the Bolognese sauce over the cooked spaghetti.
10. Garnish with grated Parmesan cheese and chopped fresh parsley.
11. Enjoy your delicious homemade Spaghetti Bolognese!

This classic Italian dish is hearty and flavorful, perfect for a satisfying meal on the road or at home. The sauce can be made ahead of time and reheated when ready to serve. Feel free to customize the recipe by adding extra vegetables or herbs according to your preference.

Turkey and Cheese Sandwich

Ingredients:

- Sliced turkey breast
- Sliced cheese (such as cheddar, Swiss, or provolone)
- Sandwich bread (whole wheat, white, or your choice)
- Lettuce leaves
- Tomato slices
- Mayonnaise or mustard (optional)
- Butter or margarine, softened (for grilling, optional)

Instructions:

1. Lay out the slices of sandwich bread on a clean surface.
2. Spread a thin layer of mayonnaise or mustard (if using) on one side of each bread slice.
3. Place a few slices of turkey breast on one bread slice.
4. Add a slice or two of cheese on top of the turkey.
5. Top with lettuce leaves and tomato slices.
6. Place another slice of bread on top to form a sandwich.
7. If desired, spread a thin layer of softened butter or margarine on the outer sides of the sandwich.
8. Heat a skillet or griddle over medium heat.
9. Place the sandwich in the skillet and grill until the bread is golden brown and the cheese is melted, about 3-4 minutes per side.
10. Alternatively, you can enjoy the sandwich cold without grilling.
11. Slice the sandwich in half diagonally.
12. Serve and enjoy your classic Turkey and Cheese Sandwich!

This simple and delicious sandwich is perfect for a quick and satisfying meal on the go. Customize the ingredients and condiments based on your preferences. Pair it with your favorite side dishes or enjoy it on its own for a tasty lunch or dinner option.

Beef Burritos

Ingredients:

- 1 lb ground beef
- 1 small onion, chopped
- 2 cloves garlic, minced
- 1 bell pepper, chopped (optional)
- 1 can (15 oz) black beans, drained and rinsed
- 1 cup cooked rice
- 1 cup shredded cheddar or Monterey Jack cheese
- 1 teaspoon chili powder
- 1/2 teaspoon ground cumin
- Salt and pepper, to taste
- 6 large flour tortillas
- Salsa, sour cream, guacamole (optional), for serving

Instructions:

1. In a large skillet, cook the ground beef over medium-high heat until browned and cooked through. Drain excess fat if needed.
2. Add the chopped onion, minced garlic, and bell pepper (if using) to the skillet. Cook for 2-3 minutes until vegetables are softened.
3. Stir in the black beans, cooked rice, chili powder, ground cumin, salt, and pepper. Mix well and cook for another 2-3 minutes to heat through.
4. Remove the skillet from heat and stir in the shredded cheese until melted and combined with the beef mixture.
5. Warm the flour tortillas in the microwave or on a skillet until pliable.
6. Spoon a portion of the beef and rice mixture onto each tortilla, slightly off-center.
7. Fold in the sides of the tortilla, then roll it up tightly to form a burrito.
8. If desired, heat a large skillet over medium heat. Place the burritos seam-side down on the skillet and cook for 2-3 minutes on each side until golden brown and crispy.
9. Serve the beef burritos with salsa, sour cream, guacamole, or your favorite toppings.
10. Enjoy your delicious homemade Beef Burritos!

These beef burritos are flavorful and satisfying, making them a great option for a quick and filling meal on the road or at home. Customize the filling with your favorite ingredients and adjust the seasoning according to your taste. Serve with your preferred toppings and enjoy!

Grilled Salmon with Vegetables

Ingredients:

- 4 salmon fillets (6 oz each), skin-on or skinless
- Salt and pepper, to taste
- 2 tablespoons olive oil
- 1 lemon, thinly sliced
- Assorted vegetables (such as bell peppers, zucchini, asparagus, cherry tomatoes)
- Fresh herbs (such as dill or parsley), for garnish

Instructions:

1. Preheat your grill to medium-high heat.
2. Season the salmon fillets with salt and pepper on both sides.
3. Drizzle the olive oil over the salmon fillets and rub to coat evenly.
4. Place the lemon slices on top of the salmon fillets.
5. Prepare the assorted vegetables by cutting them into bite-sized pieces.
6. Toss the vegetables with a little olive oil, salt, and pepper.
7. Arrange the seasoned salmon fillets and vegetables on the preheated grill.
8. Grill the salmon for about 4-5 minutes per side, depending on the thickness of the fillets, until cooked through and flaky.
9. Grill the vegetables for about 8-10 minutes, turning occasionally, until tender and lightly charred.
10. Remove the grilled salmon and vegetables from the grill.
11. Serve the grilled salmon on a platter, garnished with fresh herbs.
12. Serve the grilled vegetables alongside the salmon.
13. Squeeze fresh lemon juice over the salmon before serving, if desired.
14. Enjoy your flavorful Grilled Salmon with Vegetables!

This grilled salmon dish is healthy, delicious, and perfect for a satisfying meal on the road or at home. Feel free to customize the vegetables based on what's available or your personal preferences. Serve with a side of rice or a fresh salad for a complete and nutritious meal.

Chili Cheese Hot Dogs

Ingredients:

- 8 hot dog sausages
- 8 hot dog buns
- 2 cups chili (homemade or canned)
- 1 cup shredded cheddar cheese
- Optional toppings: diced onions, pickled jalapeños, chopped cilantro, sour cream

Instructions:

1. Preheat your grill or stovetop grill pan over medium-high heat.
2. Grill the hot dog sausages until they are nicely browned and heated through, about 5-7 minutes, turning occasionally.
3. While the hot dogs are grilling, warm the chili in a saucepan over medium heat until heated through.
4. Place the hot dog buns on the grill, cut side down, and toast lightly for 1-2 minutes.
5. Place a grilled hot dog sausage in each toasted bun.
6. Spoon a generous amount of warm chili over each hot dog.
7. Sprinkle shredded cheddar cheese over the chili.
8. Add optional toppings such as diced onions, pickled jalapeños, chopped cilantro, or sour cream according to your preference.
9. Serve immediately and enjoy your delicious Chili Cheese Hot Dogs!

These chili cheese hot dogs are a crowd-pleasing favorite and make a hearty and satisfying meal, perfect for a quick bite on the road or at home. Customize the toppings based on your taste and enjoy the bold flavors of this classic comfort food!

Tuna Salad Wrap

Ingredients:

- 2 cans (5 oz each) tuna, drained
- 1/4 cup mayonnaise
- 2 tablespoons plain Greek yogurt (or more mayonnaise)
- 1 celery stalk, finely chopped
- 1/4 cup red onion, finely chopped
- 1 tablespoon lemon juice
- Salt and pepper, to taste
- 4 large flour tortillas (10-inch diameter)
- Lettuce leaves
- Sliced tomatoes
- Sliced cucumber (optional)

Instructions:

1. In a mixing bowl, combine the drained tuna, mayonnaise, Greek yogurt, chopped celery, chopped red onion, and lemon juice.
2. Mix well until all ingredients are combined and the tuna salad is creamy.
3. Season the tuna salad with salt and pepper to taste.
4. Lay out the flour tortillas on a clean surface.
5. Place lettuce leaves on each tortilla, leaving space on one side to fold.
6. Divide the tuna salad evenly among the tortillas, spreading it in a line down the center of each tortilla.
7. Add sliced tomatoes and sliced cucumber (if using) on top of the tuna salad.
8. Fold the sides of each tortilla over the filling, then roll up tightly to form a wrap.
9. Secure the wraps with toothpicks if needed.
10. Slice the wraps in half diagonally.
11. Serve immediately and enjoy your delicious Tuna Salad Wraps!

These tuna salad wraps are easy to make and perfect for a quick and satisfying meal on the go. You can customize the ingredients based on your preference by adding other vegetables or seasonings. Enjoy these flavorful wraps for lunch or a light dinner option!

Pork Chops with Mashed Potatoes

Ingredients:

- 4 boneless pork chops
- Salt and pepper, to taste
- 2 tablespoons olive oil
- 4 large potatoes, peeled and diced
- 1/2 cup milk
- 2 tablespoons butter
- Salt and pepper, to taste
- Chopped fresh parsley, for garnish (optional)

Instructions:

1. Season the pork chops with salt and pepper on both sides.
2. In a large skillet, heat the olive oil over medium-high heat.
3. Add the pork chops to the skillet and cook for 4-5 minutes per side, or until golden brown and cooked through. The internal temperature should reach 145°F (63°C). Remove the pork chops from the skillet and set aside.
4. While the pork chops are cooking, place the diced potatoes in a pot and cover with water. Bring to a boil and cook until the potatoes are tender, about 15-20 minutes.
5. Drain the cooked potatoes and return them to the pot.
6. Add the milk and butter to the potatoes.
7. Mash the potatoes using a potato masher or fork until smooth and creamy. Season with salt and pepper to taste.
8. Serve the cooked pork chops with a generous serving of mashed potatoes.
9. Garnish with chopped fresh parsley if desired.
10. Enjoy your delicious Pork Chops with Mashed Potatoes!

This classic comfort food meal is hearty and satisfying, perfect for a cozy dinner at home. Feel free to customize the mashed potatoes with additional seasonings or add a side of vegetables for a complete meal. Enjoy!

Veggie Burger

Ingredients:

- 1 can (15 oz) black beans, drained and rinsed
- 1/2 cup cooked quinoa or brown rice
- 1/2 cup finely chopped onion
- 1/2 cup finely chopped bell pepper (any color)
- 2 cloves garlic, minced
- 1 teaspoon ground cumin
- 1 teaspoon chili powder
- Salt and pepper, to taste
- 1/4 cup breadcrumbs (or more as needed)
- 1 egg (or substitute like flaxseed meal mixed with water)
- Olive oil, for cooking
- Burger buns
- Lettuce leaves
- Sliced tomatoes
- Sliced red onion
- Optional toppings: avocado slices, cheese, mayo, ketchup, mustard

Instructions:

1. In a large bowl, mash the black beans with a fork or potato masher until mostly smooth but with some texture remaining.
2. Add cooked quinoa or brown rice, finely chopped onion, bell pepper, minced garlic, ground cumin, chili powder, salt, and pepper to the mashed black beans.
3. Mix well to combine all ingredients.
4. Add breadcrumbs and egg to the mixture. Mix until the mixture holds together and is easy to shape into patties. Add more breadcrumbs if needed to achieve the right consistency.
5. Divide the mixture into 4 equal portions and shape each portion into a burger patty.
6. Heat olive oil in a skillet over medium heat.
7. Cook the veggie burger patties for about 4-5 minutes on each side, or until golden brown and heated through.
8. Toast the burger buns lightly in the skillet or toaster.

9. Assemble the veggie burgers: Place a lettuce leaf on the bottom half of each burger bun. Top with a veggie burger patty, sliced tomatoes, and sliced red onion.
10. Add optional toppings such as avocado slices, cheese, mayo, ketchup, or mustard according to your preference.
11. Cover with the top half of the burger bun.
12. Serve immediately and enjoy your delicious homemade Veggie Burgers!

These veggie burgers are flavorful, nutritious, and perfect for a meatless meal option.

Customize the toppings and condiments based on your taste preferences and enjoy a

tasty veggie burger that's great for lunch or dinner!

Teriyaki Chicken Skewers

Ingredients:

- 1 lb boneless, skinless chicken breasts or thighs, cut into bite-sized pieces
- 1/2 cup soy sauce
- 1/4 cup mirin (Japanese sweet rice wine)
- 2 tablespoons honey or brown sugar
- 2 cloves garlic, minced
- 1-inch piece of ginger, grated
- 1 tablespoon cornstarch (optional, for thickening)
- Wooden or metal skewers
- Sliced green onions and sesame seeds, for garnish (optional)

Instructions:

1. If using wooden skewers, soak them in water for at least 30 minutes to prevent burning during grilling.
2. In a bowl, whisk together soy sauce, mirin, honey or brown sugar, minced garlic, and grated ginger to make the teriyaki marinade.
3. Reserve half of the marinade for basting later.
4. Place the chicken pieces in a shallow dish or resealable plastic bag.
5. Pour the remaining marinade over the chicken, ensuring all pieces are coated. Marinate in the refrigerator for at least 30 minutes (or up to 2 hours) to allow the flavors to develop.
6. Preheat the grill or grill pan over medium-high heat.
7. Thread the marinated chicken pieces onto the skewers, leaving a little space between each piece.
8. Grill the chicken skewers for about 5-6 minutes on each side, or until fully cooked and nicely charred.
9. While grilling, heat the reserved marinade in a small saucepan over medium heat.
10. If desired, mix cornstarch with a little water to make a slurry, then add it to the heated marinade to thicken into a sauce.
11. Brush the grilled chicken skewers with the thickened teriyaki sauce during the last few minutes of cooking.
12. Remove the chicken skewers from the grill and place them on a serving platter.
13. Garnish with sliced green onions and sesame seeds, if desired.
14. Serve hot and enjoy your flavorful Teriyaki Chicken Skewers!

These teriyaki chicken skewers are perfect for a delicious and satisfying meal, whether enjoyed at home or at a gathering. Serve them with steamed rice or a fresh salad for a complete and tasty dish. Adjust the sweetness and seasoning of the marinade according to your taste preferences.

Shrimp Fried Rice

Ingredients:

- 1 lb medium shrimp, peeled and deveined
- 3 cups cooked rice (preferably day-old and chilled)
- 2 tablespoons vegetable oil
- 3 eggs, lightly beaten
- 1 cup mixed vegetables (peas, carrots, corn, diced bell peppers)
- 4 green onions, thinly sliced
- 3 cloves garlic, minced
- 2 tablespoons soy sauce
- 1 tablespoon oyster sauce (optional)
- Salt and pepper, to taste
- Sesame oil (optional)
- Chopped fresh cilantro or parsley, for garnish

Instructions:

1. Heat 1 tablespoon of vegetable oil in a large skillet or wok over medium-high heat.
2. Add the shrimp to the skillet and cook for 2-3 minutes until pink and opaque. Remove the shrimp from the skillet and set aside.
3. In the same skillet, add the remaining tablespoon of vegetable oil.
4. Add the beaten eggs to the skillet and scramble them until just cooked. Remove the scrambled eggs from the skillet and set aside.
5. Add minced garlic and sliced green onions to the skillet. Stir-fry for about 30 seconds until fragrant.
6. Add the mixed vegetables to the skillet and stir-fry for 2-3 minutes until they start to soften.
7. Add the cooked rice to the skillet, breaking up any clumps with a spatula.
8. Return the cooked shrimp and scrambled eggs to the skillet with the rice and vegetables.
9. Drizzle soy sauce and oyster sauce (if using) over the rice mixture. Stir well to combine all ingredients.
10. Season with salt and pepper to taste. For additional flavor, drizzle a little sesame oil over the fried rice.

11. Continue to stir-fry for another 3-4 minutes until everything is heated through and well combined.
12. Remove the skillet from heat and garnish with chopped fresh cilantro or parsley.
13. Serve hot and enjoy your delicious homemade Shrimp Fried Rice!

This shrimp fried rice recipe is quick and easy to make, perfect for a flavorful meal that's great for lunch or dinner. Feel free to customize the vegetables and seasonings according to your taste preferences. Enjoy the combination of tender shrimp, fluffy rice, and savory flavors in this classic dish!

Beef Tacos

Ingredients:

- 1 lb ground beef
- 1 onion, finely chopped
- 2 cloves garlic, minced
- 1 tablespoon chili powder
- 1 teaspoon ground cumin
- 1/2 teaspoon paprika
- Salt and pepper, to taste
- 1 can (14 oz) diced tomatoes
- 1 can (8 oz) tomato sauce
- Taco shells or tortillas
- Shredded lettuce
- Diced tomatoes
- Shredded cheese (cheddar or Mexican blend)
- Sliced jalapeños (optional)
- Sour cream (optional)
- Salsa (optional)
- Chopped cilantro, for garnish (optional)
- Lime wedges, for serving

Instructions:

1. In a large skillet, cook the ground beef over medium-high heat until browned and cooked through. Drain excess fat if needed.
2. Add the chopped onion and minced garlic to the skillet. Cook for 2-3 minutes until the onion is softened.
3. Stir in the chili powder, ground cumin, paprika, salt, and pepper. Cook for another minute to toast the spices.
4. Add the diced tomatoes (with their juices) and tomato sauce to the skillet. Stir well to combine.
5. Reduce the heat to medium-low and simmer the beef mixture for 10-15 minutes, stirring occasionally, until the flavors have melded and the sauce has thickened slightly. Adjust seasoning if needed.
6. While the beef mixture is simmering, prepare your taco shells or tortillas according to package instructions.
7. Assemble the tacos: Spoon the beef mixture into taco shells or tortillas.

8. Top each taco with shredded lettuce, diced tomatoes, shredded cheese, and sliced jalapeños (if using).
9. Add sour cream and salsa as desired.
10. Garnish with chopped cilantro and serve with lime wedges on the side.
11. Enjoy your delicious homemade Beef Tacos!

These beef tacos are a classic and crowd-pleasing dish, perfect for a fun and flavorful meal with family or friends. Customize the toppings and seasonings based on your preferences, and don't forget to squeeze fresh lime juice over the tacos for a burst of citrusy flavor. Serve these tacos alongside rice and beans for a complete and satisfying Mexican-inspired meal!

Chicken Caesar Salad

Ingredients:

- 2 boneless, skinless chicken breasts
- Salt and pepper, to taste
- Olive oil
- Romaine lettuce, washed and chopped
- Caesar salad dressing (store-bought or homemade)
- Grated Parmesan cheese
- Croutons (store-bought or homemade)

Instructions:

1. Season the chicken breasts with salt and pepper on both sides.
2. Heat a drizzle of olive oil in a skillet over medium-high heat.
3. Add the seasoned chicken breasts to the skillet and cook for 6-8 minutes per side, or until cooked through and no longer pink in the center.
4. Remove the cooked chicken from the skillet and let it rest for a few minutes before slicing into thin strips.
5. In a large salad bowl, combine the chopped romaine lettuce and Caesar salad dressing. Toss well to coat the lettuce evenly with the dressing.
6. Add the sliced chicken breast strips to the salad bowl.
7. Sprinkle grated Parmesan cheese over the salad.
8. Add croutons to the salad for extra crunch.
9. Toss the salad gently to combine all ingredients.
10. Taste and adjust seasoning if needed.
11. Divide the Caesar salad among serving plates or bowls.
12. Serve immediately and enjoy your delicious Chicken Caesar Salad!

This Chicken Caesar Salad is a classic favorite that's perfect for a light and satisfying meal. Feel free to customize the salad with additional toppings such as cherry tomatoes, bacon bits, or anchovies. Serve the salad as a main dish for lunch or dinner, and enjoy the combination of crisp lettuce, tender chicken, creamy dressing, and savory Parmesan cheese!

Meatball Subs

Ingredients:

- 1 lb ground beef
- 1/2 cup breadcrumbs
- 1/4 cup grated Parmesan cheese
- 1 egg
- 2 cloves garlic, minced
- 1 teaspoon dried oregano
- Salt and pepper, to taste
- Olive oil
- 1 jar (24 oz) marinara sauce
- Sub rolls or hoagie buns
- Sliced provolone or mozzarella cheese
- Chopped fresh basil or parsley, for garnish (optional)

Instructions:

1. Preheat your oven to 375°F (190°C).
2. In a large bowl, combine the ground beef, breadcrumbs, grated Parmesan cheese, egg, minced garlic, dried oregano, salt, and pepper. Mix well until all ingredients are combined.
3. Shape the mixture into meatballs, about 1 inch in diameter.
4. Heat a drizzle of olive oil in a skillet over medium-high heat.
5. Add the meatballs to the skillet and brown them on all sides, about 4-5 minutes. You may need to do this in batches.
6. Once browned, remove the meatballs from the skillet and set them aside.
7. In the same skillet, add the marinara sauce and bring it to a simmer.
8. Return the meatballs to the skillet and coat them in the simmering marinara sauce.
9. Simmer the meatballs in the sauce for 10-15 minutes, or until they are cooked through.
10. While the meatballs are simmering, prepare your sub rolls or hoagie buns by slicing them open.
11. Place slices of provolone or mozzarella cheese inside each bun.
12. Use a slotted spoon to transfer the meatballs into the prepared buns, allowing excess sauce to drain back into the skillet.
13. Spoon some additional marinara sauce over the meatballs in each bun.

14. Close the buns and place them on a baking sheet.
15. Bake the meatball subs in the preheated oven for 5-7 minutes, or until the cheese is melted and the buns are toasted.
16. Remove from the oven and garnish with chopped fresh basil or parsley, if desired.
17. Serve hot and enjoy your delicious Meatball Subs!

These meatball subs are a satisfying and flavorful meal that's perfect for lunch or dinner. Customize the subs by adding extra toppings such as sliced onions, peppers, or your favorite condiments. Serve with a side of chips or a salad for a complete and delicious meal!

Greek Gyros

Ingredients:

- 1 lb boneless, skinless chicken breasts or thighs, thinly sliced
- 2 tablespoons olive oil
- 2 cloves garlic, minced
- 1 teaspoon dried oregano
- Salt and pepper, to taste
- Tzatziki Sauce:
    - 1 cup Greek yogurt
    - 1 cucumber, grated and squeezed to remove excess moisture
    - 2 cloves garlic, minced
    - 1 tablespoon fresh dill, chopped (or 1 teaspoon dried dill)
    - 1 tablespoon lemon juice
    - Salt and pepper, to taste
- To assemble:
    - Pita bread or flatbread
    - Sliced tomatoes
    - Sliced red onion
    - Sliced cucumbers
    - Chopped fresh parsley or dill, for garnish (optional)

Instructions:

1. In a bowl, combine the thinly sliced chicken with olive oil, minced garlic, dried oregano, salt, and pepper. Mix well to coat the chicken evenly.
2. Heat a skillet or grill pan over medium-high heat.
3. Cook the marinated chicken slices in the skillet for 5-6 minutes, or until cooked through and slightly charred. Remove from heat and set aside.
4. To make the tzatziki sauce, combine Greek yogurt, grated cucumber, minced garlic, chopped dill, lemon juice, salt, and pepper in a bowl. Mix well until smooth and creamy. Adjust seasoning to taste.
5. Warm the pita bread or flatbread in the skillet or microwave.
6. To assemble the gyros, spread a generous amount of tzatziki sauce on each warmed pita bread.
7. Top with sliced cooked chicken, sliced tomatoes, sliced red onion, and sliced cucumbers.
8. Garnish with chopped fresh parsley or dill, if desired.

9. Roll up the pita bread to enclose the filling and secure with foil or parchment paper.
10. Serve immediately and enjoy your flavorful Greek Gyros!

These Greek gyros are a delicious and satisfying meal filled with Mediterranean flavors. Customize the gyros with additional toppings such as feta cheese, olives, or hot sauce according to your preference. Serve with a side of Greek salad or fries for a complete and hearty meal!

Macaroni and Cheese

Ingredients:

- 8 oz elbow macaroni (or any pasta shape you prefer)
- 4 tablespoons butter
- 1/4 cup all-purpose flour
- 2 cups milk
- 2 cups shredded sharp cheddar cheese
- Salt and pepper, to taste
- Optional add-ins: cooked bacon bits, diced ham, chopped broccoli, diced tomatoes

Instructions:

1. Cook the elbow macaroni according to package instructions until al dente. Drain and set aside.
2. In a large pot or skillet, melt the butter over medium heat.
3. Whisk in the flour to create a roux. Cook for 1-2 minutes, stirring constantly, until the roux is golden and fragrant.
4. Gradually whisk in the milk, stirring constantly to avoid lumps.
5. Continue cooking and stirring until the sauce thickens and starts to bubble.
6. Reduce the heat to low and stir in the shredded cheddar cheese until melted and smooth.
7. Season the cheese sauce with salt and pepper to taste.
8. Add the cooked macaroni to the cheese sauce, stirring until the pasta is well coated.
9. If desired, stir in optional add-ins such as cooked bacon bits, diced ham, chopped broccoli, or diced tomatoes.
10. Cook for an additional 2-3 minutes over low heat to heat through and combine flavors.
11. Remove from heat and serve the macaroni and cheese immediately.
12. Enjoy your creamy and cheesy Macaroni and Cheese!

This classic macaroni and cheese recipe is quick and easy to make, perfect for a comforting and satisfying meal. Customize the dish by adding your favorite ingredients or spices to make it your own. Serve as a main dish or side dish alongside a salad or vegetables for a delicious meal that everyone will love!

Hawaiian Pizza

Ingredients:

- 1 pre-made pizza dough (store-bought or homemade)
- 1/2 cup pizza sauce
- 1 1/2 cups shredded mozzarella cheese
- 1/2 cup diced cooked ham or Canadian bacon
- 1/2 cup pineapple chunks (fresh or canned, drained)
- Red pepper flakes (optional, for heat)
- Fresh basil leaves, chopped (optional, for garnish)

Instructions:

1. Preheat your oven to the temperature specified on the pizza dough package (usually around 425°F or 220°C).
2. Roll out the pizza dough on a lightly floured surface to your desired thickness.
3. Transfer the rolled-out dough to a pizza pan or baking sheet.
4. Spread pizza sauce evenly over the dough, leaving a small border around the edges for the crust.
5. Sprinkle shredded mozzarella cheese over the sauce-covered dough.
6. Distribute diced ham or Canadian bacon and pineapple chunks evenly over the cheese.
7. If you like a bit of heat, sprinkle some red pepper flakes over the toppings.
8. Place the pizza in the preheated oven and bake according to the dough package instructions, typically for 12-15 minutes or until the crust is golden and the cheese is bubbly and melted.
9. Remove the pizza from the oven and let it cool slightly.
10. Sprinkle chopped fresh basil leaves over the hot pizza for a burst of flavor and freshness.
11. Slice the Hawaiian pizza into wedges or squares.
12. Serve hot and enjoy your delicious homemade Hawaiian Pizza!

This Hawaiian pizza combines the savory flavors of ham or Canadian bacon with the sweet and tangy taste of pineapple for a delightful tropical twist. Customize the toppings based on your preference and enjoy this classic pizza as a tasty meal for lunch, dinner, or even as a party appetizer!

BLT Sandwich

Ingredients:

- 8 slices of bread (white, whole wheat, or your choice)
- 1 lb bacon, cooked until crispy
- 2 large tomatoes, sliced
- Iceberg lettuce leaves
- Mayonnaise
- Salt and pepper, to taste

Instructions:

1. Cook the bacon in a skillet over medium heat until crispy. Drain on paper towels and set aside.
2. Toast the bread slices in a toaster or under the broiler until golden brown.
3. Spread a thin layer of mayonnaise on one side of each bread slice.
4. Arrange iceberg lettuce leaves on 4 of the bread slices.
5. Top the lettuce with sliced tomatoes.
6. Season the tomatoes with salt and pepper to taste.
7. Place crispy bacon slices on top of the tomatoes.
8. Place the remaining bread slices on top to form sandwiches.
9. Cut the sandwiches in half diagonally.
10. Serve immediately and enjoy your classic BLT Sandwich!

This BLT (Bacon, Lettuce, and Tomato) sandwich is a timeless favorite, perfect for a quick and delicious meal. Customize the sandwich by adding avocado slices, extra mayo, or different types of lettuce for variation. Serve with a side of potato chips or a pickle for a classic lunchtime treat!

Beef and Broccoli Stir-Fry

Ingredients:

- 1 lb flank steak or sirloin steak, thinly sliced against the grain
- 2 tablespoons soy sauce
- 1 tablespoon oyster sauce
- 1 tablespoon hoisin sauce
- 1 tablespoon rice vinegar
- 1 tablespoon brown sugar
- 2 cloves garlic, minced
- 1-inch piece of ginger, grated
- 2 tablespoons vegetable oil
- 1 head broccoli, cut into florets
- 1 bell pepper, thinly sliced (optional)
- Cooked rice or noodles, for serving

Instructions:

1. In a bowl, combine the sliced beef with soy sauce, oyster sauce, hoisin sauce, rice vinegar, brown sugar, minced garlic, and grated ginger. Mix well and let it marinate for at least 15-30 minutes.
2. Heat 1 tablespoon of vegetable oil in a large skillet or wok over high heat.
3. Add the marinated beef to the skillet in a single layer. Cook for 1-2 minutes without stirring to allow the beef to sear and brown on one side. Then stir-fry for another 1-2 minutes until the beef is cooked to your desired doneness. Remove the beef from the skillet and set aside.
4. Add the remaining tablespoon of vegetable oil to the skillet.
5. Add the broccoli florets (and sliced bell pepper, if using) to the skillet. Stir-fry for 3-4 minutes until the broccoli is tender-crisp.
6. Return the cooked beef to the skillet with the broccoli.
7. Stir everything together and cook for another minute to heat through.
8. Taste and adjust seasoning if needed.
9. Serve the beef and broccoli stir-fry over cooked rice or noodles.
10. Enjoy your delicious Beef and Broccoli Stir-Fry!

This beef and broccoli stir-fry is quick and easy to make, perfect for a flavorful and nutritious meal. Customize the stir-fry with your favorite vegetables or add additional seasonings according to your taste. Serve hot and enjoy the tender beef and crisp broccoli in a savory sauce over rice or noodles!

Italian Sausage Penne

Ingredients:

- 1 lb Italian sausage (sweet or spicy), casings removed
- 1 onion, chopped
- 3 cloves garlic, minced
- 1 can (14.5 oz) diced tomatoes
- 1 can (8 oz) tomato sauce
- 1 teaspoon dried basil
- 1 teaspoon dried oregano
- Salt and pepper, to taste
- 12 oz penne pasta
- Grated Parmesan cheese, for serving
- Chopped fresh parsley, for garnish (optional)

Instructions:

1. In a large skillet or pot, cook the Italian sausage over medium-high heat, breaking it up with a wooden spoon, until browned and cooked through. Remove any excess fat.
2. Add the chopped onion to the skillet and cook for 3-4 minutes until softened.
3. Stir in the minced garlic and cook for another 1 minute until fragrant.
4. Add the diced tomatoes (with their juices), tomato sauce, dried basil, dried oregano, salt, and pepper to the skillet. Stir to combine.
5. Reduce the heat to medium-low and let the sauce simmer for about 15-20 minutes, stirring occasionally, to allow the flavors to meld and the sauce to thicken slightly.
6. While the sauce is simmering, cook the penne pasta according to package instructions until al dente. Drain the pasta and set aside.
7. Add the cooked penne pasta to the skillet with the sauce and toss to coat the pasta evenly.
8. Taste and adjust seasoning if needed.
9. Serve the Italian sausage penne hot, garnished with grated Parmesan cheese and chopped fresh parsley if desired.
10. Enjoy your flavorful Italian Sausage Penne pasta dish!

This Italian sausage penne recipe is hearty, comforting, and perfect for a satisfying dinner. Serve with a side of garlic bread or a fresh green salad for a complete meal. Feel free to customize the dish by adding extra vegetables such as bell peppers or spinach to the sauce. Enjoy the delicious flavors of Italian sausage and savory tomato sauce with tender penne pasta!

Egg Salad Wrap

Ingredients:

- 6 hard-boiled eggs, peeled and chopped
- 1/4 cup mayonnaise
- 1 tablespoon Dijon mustard
- 2 tablespoons finely chopped celery
- 2 tablespoons finely chopped green onion
- Salt and pepper, to taste
- 4 large flour tortillas (10-inch diameter)
- Lettuce leaves
- Sliced tomatoes (optional)

Instructions:

1. In a mixing bowl, combine the chopped hard-boiled eggs, mayonnaise, Dijon mustard, chopped celery, and chopped green onion.
2. Mix well until all ingredients are thoroughly combined and the egg salad is creamy.
3. Season the egg salad with salt and pepper to taste.
4. Lay out the flour tortillas on a clean surface.
5. Place lettuce leaves on each tortilla, leaving space on one side to fold.
6. Divide the egg salad evenly among the tortillas, spreading it in a line down the center of each tortilla.
7. Add sliced tomatoes on top of the egg salad, if using.
8. Fold the sides of each tortilla over the filling, then roll up tightly to form a wrap.
9. Secure the wraps with toothpicks if needed.
10. Slice the wraps in half diagonally.
11. Serve immediately and enjoy your delicious Egg Salad Wraps!

These egg salad wraps are perfect for a quick and satisfying meal, whether enjoyed at home or packed for lunch on the go. Customize the wraps by adding extra vegetables or herbs to the egg salad, or serve with a side of chips or fresh fruit for a complete and tasty meal. Enjoy the creamy and flavorful egg salad wrapped in a soft tortilla!

Chicken Quesadillas

Ingredients:

- 2 cups cooked chicken, shredded or diced
- 1 bell pepper, diced
- 1 small onion, diced
- 1 cup shredded cheese (cheddar, Monterey Jack, or a blend)
- 4 large flour tortillas
- 2 tablespoons olive oil or melted butter
- Salt and pepper, to taste
- Optional toppings: sour cream, salsa, guacamole, chopped cilantro

Instructions:

1. In a skillet, heat 1 tablespoon of olive oil over medium heat.
2. Add diced bell pepper and onion to the skillet. Cook for 3-4 minutes until softened.
3. Add cooked chicken to the skillet and season with salt and pepper. Stir to combine and cook for another 2-3 minutes until heated through.
4. Remove the skillet from heat and set aside.
5. Place a large skillet or griddle over medium heat.
6. Brush one side of a flour tortilla with olive oil or melted butter.
7. Place the tortilla oil/butter side down on the skillet.
8. Spread a portion of the chicken mixture evenly over half of the tortilla.
9. Sprinkle shredded cheese over the chicken mixture.
10. Fold the tortilla in half over the filling, pressing down gently with a spatula.
11. Cook the quesadilla for 2-3 minutes on each side, or until golden brown and crispy, and the cheese is melted.
12. Remove the cooked quesadilla from the skillet and repeat the process with the remaining tortillas and filling.
13. Slice the quesadillas into wedges using a pizza cutter or knife.
14. Serve hot with optional toppings such as sour cream, salsa, guacamole, or chopped cilantro.
15. Enjoy your delicious Chicken Quesadillas!

These chicken quesadillas are a crowd-pleasing favorite and make a quick and satisfying meal for lunch or dinner. Customize the filling with your favorite vegetables, add jalapeños for heat, or use different types of cheese for variation. Serve with your preferred toppings and enjoy the gooey, cheesy goodness of these homemade quesadillas!

Sloppy Joes

Ingredients:

- 1 lb ground beef (or ground turkey)
- 1 small onion, finely chopped
- 1 green bell pepper, finely chopped
- 2 cloves garlic, minced
- 1 cup ketchup
- 2 tablespoons tomato paste
- 1 tablespoon Worcestershire sauce
- 1 tablespoon brown sugar
- 1 teaspoon chili powder
- Salt and pepper, to taste
- Hamburger buns

Instructions:

1. In a large skillet or saucepan, brown the ground beef over medium-high heat, breaking it up with a spoon as it cooks.
2. Add the chopped onion and bell pepper to the skillet with the browned beef. Cook for 3-4 minutes until the vegetables start to soften.
3. Add the minced garlic and cook for another 1 minute until fragrant.
4. Stir in the ketchup, tomato paste, Worcestershire sauce, brown sugar, chili powder, salt, and pepper.
5. Reduce the heat to medium-low and let the mixture simmer for 10-15 minutes, stirring occasionally, to allow the flavors to meld and the sauce to thicken.
6. Taste and adjust seasoning if needed.
7. While the mixture is simmering, toast the hamburger buns under the broiler or in a toaster until golden brown.
8. Spoon the sloppy joe mixture onto the bottom halves of the toasted hamburger buns.
9. Top with the other halves of the hamburger buns to complete the sandwiches.
10. Serve immediately and enjoy your homemade Sloppy Joes!

These Sloppy Joes are a classic and comforting meal that's perfect for a quick and easy dinner. Serve with a side of potato chips, coleslaw, or pickles for a delicious and satisfying meal. Enjoy the savory and tangy flavors of these sloppy joe sandwiches!

Asian Noodle Salad

Ingredients:

- 8 oz thin spaghetti or soba noodles
- 1 cup shredded cooked chicken (rotisserie chicken works well)
- 1 red bell pepper, thinly sliced
- 1 cucumber, thinly sliced
- 1 carrot, julienned or shredded
- 1/2 cup shredded cabbage
- 1/4 cup chopped green onions
- 1/4 cup chopped fresh cilantro or parsley
- 1/4 cup chopped roasted peanuts or cashews (optional, for garnish)

For the Dressing:

- 1/4 cup soy sauce
- 3 tablespoons rice vinegar
- 2 tablespoons sesame oil
- 1 tablespoon honey or brown sugar
- 2 cloves garlic, minced
- 1 teaspoon grated ginger
- Red pepper flakes, to taste (optional)

Instructions:

1. Cook the noodles according to package instructions until al dente. Drain and rinse under cold water to stop the cooking process. Set aside.
2. In a large bowl, combine the cooked noodles, shredded chicken, sliced bell pepper, sliced cucumber, julienned carrot, shredded cabbage, chopped green onions, and chopped cilantro or parsley.
3. In a separate small bowl, whisk together the soy sauce, rice vinegar, sesame oil, honey or brown sugar, minced garlic, grated ginger, and red pepper flakes (if using) to make the dressing.
4. Pour the dressing over the noodle and vegetable mixture. Toss well to coat everything evenly with the dressing.
5. Taste and adjust seasoning if needed.

6. Cover the bowl and refrigerate the Asian noodle salad for at least 30 minutes to allow the flavors to meld.
7. Before serving, give the salad a final toss.
8. Garnish with chopped roasted peanuts or cashews, if desired.
9. Serve chilled and enjoy your refreshing and flavorful Asian Noodle Salad!

This Asian noodle salad is light, colorful, and packed with fresh vegetables and savory flavors. It makes a delicious main dish for lunch or dinner, and leftovers can be enjoyed as a cold salad the next day. Customize the salad by adding other vegetables like snap peas, bean sprouts, or edamame. It's a versatile and satisfying dish that's perfect for warm weather or any time you're craving a healthy and tasty meal!

Vegetable Soup

Ingredients:

- 2 tablespoons olive oil
- 1 onion, diced
- 2 carrots, diced
- 2 celery stalks, diced
- 2 cloves garlic, minced
- 1 zucchini, diced
- 1 yellow squash, diced
- 1 bell pepper (any color), diced
- 1 can (14.5 oz) diced tomatoes
- 6 cups vegetable broth (or chicken broth)
- 1 teaspoon dried thyme
- 1 teaspoon dried oregano
- Salt and pepper, to taste
- 1 cup cooked beans (such as kidney beans or chickpeas), drained and rinsed (optional)
- 2 cups fresh spinach or kale, chopped
- Fresh parsley or basil, chopped (for garnish)

Instructions:

1. In a large pot or Dutch oven, heat the olive oil over medium heat.
2. Add the diced onion, carrots, and celery to the pot. Cook for 5-7 minutes, stirring occasionally, until the vegetables start to soften.
3. Add the minced garlic, diced zucchini, yellow squash, and diced bell pepper to the pot. Cook for another 3-4 minutes.
4. Stir in the diced tomatoes (with their juices), vegetable broth, dried thyme, dried oregano, salt, and pepper.
5. Bring the soup to a simmer. Reduce the heat to low, cover the pot, and let it simmer for 20-25 minutes, or until all the vegetables are tender.
6. If using cooked beans, add them to the soup during the last 5 minutes of cooking to heat through.
7. Stir in the chopped spinach or kale and cook for an additional 1-2 minutes until wilted.
8. Taste and adjust seasoning with salt and pepper if needed.

9. Remove the pot from heat.
10. Ladle the vegetable soup into bowls.
11. Garnish with chopped fresh parsley or basil.
12. Serve hot and enjoy your comforting and nutritious Vegetable Soup!

This vegetable soup is a wholesome and satisfying dish that's perfect for a light lunch or dinner. It's packed with a variety of colorful vegetables and can be easily customized with your favorite additions or substitutions. Serve with crusty bread or a side salad for a complete meal. Enjoy the delicious flavors of this homemade vegetable soup!

Pulled BBQ Chicken Sandwich

Ingredients:

- 1 lb boneless, skinless chicken breasts
- Salt and pepper, to taste
- 1 cup barbecue sauce (store-bought or homemade)
- 1/2 cup chicken broth or water
- 4 sandwich buns (such as hamburger buns or ciabatta rolls)
- Coleslaw (optional, for topping)

Instructions:

1. Season the chicken breasts with salt and pepper on both sides.
2. In a slow cooker or crockpot, combine the seasoned chicken breasts, barbecue sauce, and chicken broth or water.
3. Cover and cook on low for 4-6 hours, or until the chicken is tender and can be easily shredded with a fork.
4. Once the chicken is cooked, use two forks to shred the chicken directly in the slow cooker, mixing it with the barbecue sauce.
5. Toast the sandwich buns if desired.
6. Spoon the pulled BBQ chicken onto the bottom halves of the sandwich buns.
7. Top with coleslaw if using.
8. Place the top halves of the sandwich buns over the chicken to complete the sandwiches.
9. Serve immediately and enjoy your delicious Pulled BBQ Chicken Sandwiches!

These pulled BBQ chicken sandwiches are perfect for a quick and flavorful meal. The tender and saucy shredded chicken pairs perfectly with the soft sandwich buns. Customize your sandwiches with additional toppings like pickles, sliced onions, or cheese. Serve with a side of potato chips or a green salad for a satisfying lunch or dinner option!

Buffalo Chicken Wings

Ingredients:

- 2 lbs chicken wings, drumettes and flats separated
- Salt and pepper, to taste
- 1/2 cup all-purpose flour
- 1 teaspoon garlic powder
- 1 teaspoon paprika
- Vegetable oil, for frying

For Buffalo Sauce:

- 1/2 cup hot sauce (such as Frank's RedHot)
- 1/4 cup unsalted butter
- 1 tablespoon honey (optional, for sweetness)
- 1 teaspoon Worcestershire sauce
- 1 teaspoon garlic powder
- Blue cheese dressing or ranch dressing, for serving
- Celery sticks, for serving

Instructions:

1. Pat the chicken wings dry with paper towels and season with salt and pepper.
2. In a shallow bowl, combine the flour, garlic powder, and paprika.
3. Dredge the chicken wings in the seasoned flour, shaking off any excess.
4. In a deep skillet or Dutch oven, heat enough vegetable oil to cover the wings over medium-high heat until it reaches 350°F (175°C).
5. Carefully add the chicken wings to the hot oil in batches, without overcrowding the pan. Fry for about 10-12 minutes, turning occasionally, until golden brown and cooked through.
6. Remove the fried wings with a slotted spoon and drain on a paper towel-lined plate. Repeat with the remaining wings.
7. In a saucepan, combine the hot sauce, unsalted butter, honey (if using), Worcestershire sauce, and garlic powder over low heat. Stir until the butter is melted and the sauce is smooth.
8. Toss the fried chicken wings in the buffalo sauce until evenly coated.

9. Serve the buffalo chicken wings hot with blue cheese dressing or ranch dressing for dipping.
10. Garnish with celery sticks on the side.
11. Enjoy your spicy and flavorful Buffalo Chicken Wings!

These Buffalo Chicken Wings are a classic favorite for parties or game day gatherings. They are crispy, spicy, and packed with flavor. Adjust the level of heat by adding more or less hot sauce according to your preference. Serve with your favorite dipping sauce and enjoy this delicious finger food with friends and family!

Beef Kebabs

Ingredients:

- 1 lb beef sirloin or top round, cut into 1-inch cubes
- 1 bell pepper, cut into chunks
- 1 red onion, cut into chunks
- Cherry tomatoes
- Wooden or metal skewers
- Salt and pepper, to taste
- Marinade (optional):
    - 1/4 cup olive oil
    - 2 tablespoons soy sauce
    - 2 tablespoons Worcestershire sauce
    - 2 cloves garlic, minced
    - 1 teaspoon dried oregano
    - 1 teaspoon paprika
    - Juice of 1 lemon (optional)

Instructions:

1. If using wooden skewers, soak them in water for at least 30 minutes to prevent burning.
2. In a bowl, combine the olive oil, soy sauce, Worcestershire sauce, minced garlic, dried oregano, paprika, and lemon juice (if using) to make the marinade.
3. Season the beef cubes with salt and pepper.
4. Place the beef cubes in the marinade, tossing to coat evenly. Cover and refrigerate for at least 30 minutes, or up to 4 hours.
5. Preheat your grill or broiler to medium-high heat.
6. Thread the marinated beef cubes onto skewers, alternating with bell pepper chunks, red onion chunks, and cherry tomatoes.
7. Grill the beef kebabs for 8-10 minutes, turning occasionally, until the beef is cooked to your desired doneness and the vegetables are tender and slightly charred.
8. Remove the beef kebabs from the grill and let them rest for a few minutes.
9. Serve the beef kebabs hot with rice, salad, or grilled vegetables.
10. Enjoy your delicious and flavorful Beef Kebabs!

These beef kebabs are perfect for outdoor grilling or indoor broiling. The marinade adds wonderful flavor to the beef and vegetables, making these kebabs a crowd-pleasing dish for any occasion. Customize the vegetables based on your preference, and serve with your favorite sides for a complete and satisfying meal!

Fish Tacos

Ingredients:

- 1 lb firm white fish fillets (such as cod, tilapia, or mahi-mahi)
- Salt and pepper, to taste
- 1 teaspoon chili powder
- 1/2 teaspoon cumin
- 1/2 teaspoon paprika
- 1 tablespoon olive oil
- Corn or flour tortillas
- Cabbage slaw (recipe below)
- Sliced avocado, for serving
- Fresh cilantro, chopped, for serving
- Lime wedges, for serving

For Cabbage Slaw:

- 2 cups shredded cabbage (green or purple)
- 1 carrot, grated
- 1/4 cup chopped cilantro
- 2 tablespoons mayonnaise
- 1 tablespoon lime juice
- Salt and pepper, to taste

Instructions:

1. In a small bowl, mix together the chili powder, cumin, paprika, salt, and pepper.
2. Pat the fish fillets dry with paper towels and season both sides with the spice mixture.
3. Heat the olive oil in a skillet over medium-high heat.
4. Add the seasoned fish fillets to the skillet and cook for 3-4 minutes per side, or until the fish is cooked through and flakes easily with a fork.
5. Remove the fish from the skillet and flake into bite-sized pieces using a fork.
6. To make the cabbage slaw, combine the shredded cabbage, grated carrot, chopped cilantro, mayonnaise, lime juice, salt, and pepper in a bowl. Mix well to coat the cabbage evenly with the dressing.
7. Warm the tortillas in a dry skillet or microwave.
8. Assemble the fish tacos by placing some flaked fish on each tortilla.

9. Top with cabbage slaw, sliced avocado, and chopped fresh cilantro.
10. Serve the fish tacos with lime wedges on the side.
11. Enjoy your delicious and flavorful Fish Tacos!

These fish tacos are fresh, flavorful, and perfect for a quick and satisfying meal. Customize your tacos with additional toppings such as salsa, diced onions, or hot sauce. Serve with a side of Mexican rice, beans, or tortilla chips for a complete and delicious dinner!

Pesto Pasta with Grilled Chicken

Ingredients:

- 8 oz pasta (such as penne or fusilli)
- 2 boneless, skinless chicken breasts
- Salt and pepper, to taste
- Olive oil, for grilling
- 1/2 cup prepared basil pesto (store-bought or homemade)
- 1/4 cup grated Parmesan cheese
- Cherry tomatoes, halved (optional)
- Fresh basil leaves, chopped (for garnish)

Instructions:

1. Cook the pasta according to package instructions until al dente. Drain and set aside.
2. Preheat a grill or grill pan over medium-high heat.
3. Season the chicken breasts with salt and pepper.
4. Drizzle olive oil over the chicken breasts and rub to coat evenly.
5. Grill the chicken breasts for 6-8 minutes per side, or until cooked through and nicely charred. The internal temperature should reach 165°F (74°C). Remove from the grill and let them rest for a few minutes before slicing.
6. In a large bowl, toss the cooked pasta with basil pesto until well coated.
7. Add grated Parmesan cheese to the pasta and toss again to combine.
8. Slice the grilled chicken breasts into strips.
9. Arrange the pesto pasta on plates or in bowls.
10. Top the pasta with sliced grilled chicken.
11. If desired, garnish with halved cherry tomatoes and chopped fresh basil leaves.
12. Serve immediately and enjoy your delicious Pesto Pasta with Grilled Chicken!

This Pesto Pasta with Grilled Chicken is a simple and satisfying meal that's bursting with flavor. The combination of creamy basil pesto, tender grilled chicken, and al dente pasta creates a perfect harmony of textures and tastes. Serve as a main dish for lunch or dinner, and customize with additional vegetables or herbs according to your preference. Enjoy this delicious and comforting pasta dish!

Ham and Cheese Panini

Ingredients:

- 4 slices of sandwich bread (such as ciabatta, sourdough, or multigrain)
- 4 slices of deli ham
- 4 slices of cheese (such as Swiss, cheddar, or provolone)
- Butter or olive oil, for grilling

Instructions:

1. Preheat a panini press, grill pan, or skillet over medium heat.
2. Lay out the slices of bread on a clean surface.
3. Place a slice of cheese on each slice of bread.
4. Layer the ham slices on top of the cheese.
5. Top with another slice of cheese.
6. Place another slice of bread on top to form sandwiches.
7. Brush the outsides of the sandwiches with melted butter or olive oil.
8. Place the sandwiches on the preheated panini press, grill pan, or skillet.
9. If using a panini press, close the lid and grill for 3-4 minutes, or until the bread is golden brown and crispy, and the cheese is melted.
10. If using a grill pan or skillet, grill the sandwiches for 3-4 minutes on each side, pressing down gently with a spatula, until the bread is golden brown and the cheese is melted.
11. Remove the grilled sandwiches from the panini press, grill pan, or skillet.
12. Let them cool for a minute, then slice in half diagonally.
13. Serve hot and enjoy your delicious Ham and Cheese Panini!

This Ham and Cheese Panini is a classic and comforting sandwich that's perfect for a quick and satisfying meal. Customize the panini by adding additional ingredients such as sliced tomatoes, caramelized onions, or mustard. Serve with a side of pickles, potato chips, or a simple green salad for a complete lunch or dinner. Enjoy the warm and melty goodness of this tasty panini!

Beef and Bean Burritos

Ingredients:

- 1 lb ground beef
- 1 onion, diced
- 2 cloves garlic, minced
- 1 can (15 oz) refried beans
- 1 can (4 oz) diced green chilies
- 1 teaspoon chili powder
- 1 teaspoon cumin
- Salt and pepper, to taste
- 8 large flour tortillas
- Shredded cheese (cheddar, Monterey Jack, or Mexican blend)
- Optional toppings: chopped lettuce, diced tomatoes, sliced jalapeños, sour cream, salsa

Instructions:

1. In a large skillet, cook the ground beef over medium-high heat until browned and cooked through.
2. Add the diced onion and minced garlic to the skillet with the cooked beef. Cook for 3-4 minutes until the onion is softened.
3. Stir in the refried beans, diced green chilies, chili powder, cumin, salt, and pepper. Mix well until everything is heated through and well combined.
4. Warm the flour tortillas in a dry skillet or microwave to make them pliable.
5. Spoon a portion of the beef and bean mixture onto each tortilla, spreading it in a line down the center.
6. Sprinkle shredded cheese over the beef and bean mixture.
7. Fold the sides of each tortilla over the filling, then roll up tightly to form burritos.
8. Place the burritos seam-side down on a baking sheet.
9. If desired, sprinkle additional cheese on top of the burritos.
10. Bake in a preheated oven at 350°F (175°C) for 10-12 minutes, or until the burritos are heated through and the cheese is melted.
11. Remove the baked burritos from the oven.
12. Serve hot with optional toppings such as chopped lettuce, diced tomatoes, sliced jalapeños, sour cream, and salsa.
13. Enjoy your delicious Beef and Bean Burritos!

These Beef and Bean Burritos are hearty and flavorful, perfect for a quick and satisfying dinner. Customize the burritos with your favorite toppings and serve with rice, chips, or a side salad for a complete meal. They also make great leftovers for lunch the next day. Enjoy the delicious combination of seasoned beef, creamy refried beans, and melted cheese wrapped in a warm tortilla!

Caesar Salad with Grilled Shrimp

Ingredients:

- 1 lb large shrimp, peeled and deveined
- Salt and pepper, to taste
- Olive oil, for grilling
- 1 head of romaine lettuce, washed and chopped
- Caesar salad dressing (store-bought or homemade)
- Grated Parmesan cheese, for topping
- Croutons, for topping

For Caesar Salad Dressing (optional, if making from scratch):

- 1/2 cup mayonnaise
- 2 tablespoons grated Parmesan cheese
- 2 tablespoons fresh lemon juice
- 1 tablespoon Dijon mustard
- 2 cloves garlic, minced
- 1 anchovy fillet, minced (or 1 teaspoon anchovy paste)
- Salt and pepper, to taste
- Olive oil (about 1/4 cup), for thinning the dressing

Instructions:

1. Preheat a grill or grill pan over medium-high heat.
2. Season the shrimp with salt, pepper, and a drizzle of olive oil.
3. Thread the seasoned shrimp onto skewers, if using.
4. Grill the shrimp for 2-3 minutes per side, or until pink and opaque. Remove from the grill and set aside.
5. In a large bowl, toss the chopped romaine lettuce with Caesar salad dressing until well coated.
6. Divide the dressed romaine lettuce onto serving plates.
7. Top each salad with grilled shrimp.
8. Sprinkle grated Parmesan cheese and croutons over the salads.
9. Serve immediately and enjoy your delicious Caesar Salad with Grilled Shrimp!

For Caesar Salad Dressing (if making from scratch):

1. In a small bowl, whisk together the mayonnaise, grated Parmesan cheese, fresh lemon juice, Dijon mustard, minced garlic, and minced anchovy fillet (or anchovy paste).
2. Season with salt and pepper to taste.
3. Gradually whisk in olive oil until the dressing reaches your desired consistency.
4. Adjust seasoning and tanginess by adding more lemon juice or Parmesan cheese if needed.
5. Use immediately or store in the refrigerator for up to a week.

This Caesar Salad with Grilled Shrimp is a delightful combination of crisp romaine lettuce, flavorful Caesar dressing, and juicy grilled shrimp. It makes a perfect light meal or appetizer, especially during warmer months. Feel free to customize the salad with additional toppings such as cherry tomatoes, avocado slices, or extra Parmesan cheese. Enjoy the fresh and satisfying flavors of this delicious salad!

Veggie Stir-Fried Rice

Ingredients:

- 3 cups cooked rice (preferably day-old rice)
- 2 tablespoons vegetable oil
- 2 cloves garlic, minced
- 1 onion, finely chopped
- 1 bell pepper, diced
- 1 carrot, diced
- 1 cup frozen peas, thawed
- 2 eggs, beaten
- 3 tablespoons soy sauce (or to taste)
- 1 tablespoon oyster sauce (optional)
- Salt and pepper, to taste
- Green onions, chopped (for garnish)

Instructions:

1. Heat vegetable oil in a large skillet or wok over medium-high heat.
2. Add minced garlic and chopped onion to the skillet. Stir-fry for 1-2 minutes until fragrant and onions are translucent.
3. Add diced bell pepper and carrot to the skillet. Stir-fry for another 3-4 minutes until vegetables are tender-crisp.
4. Push the vegetables to one side of the skillet and pour beaten eggs onto the empty side. Allow the eggs to set slightly, then scramble them until cooked through.
5. Mix the cooked vegetables and scrambled eggs together in the skillet.
6. Add cooked rice and thawed peas to the skillet. Stir well to combine all ingredients.
7. Pour soy sauce and oyster sauce (if using) over the rice mixture. Stir continuously to evenly distribute the sauces and seasonings.
8. Cook for another 3-4 minutes, stirring frequently, until the rice is heated through and slightly crispy.
9. Taste and adjust seasoning with salt, pepper, and additional soy sauce if needed.
10. Remove the skillet from heat.
11. Garnish with chopped green onions.
12. Serve hot and enjoy your delicious Vegetable Stir-Fried Rice!

This Vegetable Stir-Fried Rice is a quick, flavorful, and versatile dish that's perfect for using up leftover rice and vegetables. Customize the stir-fried rice by adding or substituting different vegetables such as broccoli, snow peas, or bean sprouts. You can also add cooked chicken, shrimp, or tofu for extra protein. Enjoy this satisfying and tasty stir-fried rice as a main dish or side dish for lunch or dinner!

Chicken Enchiladas

Ingredients:

- 2 cups cooked, shredded chicken (rotisserie chicken works well)
- 1 onion, finely chopped
- 2 cloves garlic, minced
- 1 bell pepper, diced
- 1 can (15 oz) black beans, drained and rinsed
- 1 can (4 oz) diced green chilies
- 1 cup corn kernels (fresh, frozen, or canned)
- 1 teaspoon ground cumin
- 1 teaspoon chili powder
- Salt and pepper, to taste
- 2 cups shredded cheese (cheddar, Monterey Jack, or Mexican blend)
- 10-12 corn or flour tortillas
- Enchilada sauce (store-bought or homemade)
- Chopped fresh cilantro, for garnish
- Sliced jalapeños, for garnish (optional)
- Sour cream, for serving (optional)

Instructions:

1. Preheat the oven to 375°F (190°C). Grease a 9x13-inch baking dish with cooking spray or oil.
2. In a large skillet, heat a bit of oil over medium heat.
3. Add chopped onion and diced bell pepper to the skillet. Cook for 3-4 minutes until softened.
4. Add minced garlic and cook for another 1 minute until fragrant.
5. Stir in the shredded chicken, black beans, diced green chilies, corn kernels, ground cumin, chili powder, salt, and pepper. Mix well to combine and cook for a few more minutes until heated through.
6. Remove the skillet from heat.
7. Warm the tortillas briefly in the microwave or on a skillet until they are soft and pliable.
8. Spoon a portion of the chicken and vegetable mixture onto each tortilla, then sprinkle some shredded cheese over the filling.
9. Roll up the tortillas tightly and place them seam-side down in the prepared baking dish.

10. Pour enchilada sauce over the rolled tortillas, covering them evenly.
11. Sprinkle the remaining shredded cheese over the top of the enchiladas.
12. Cover the baking dish with aluminum foil.
13. Bake in the preheated oven for 20-25 minutes, or until the cheese is melted and bubbly.
14. Remove the foil and bake for an additional 5 minutes to lightly brown the cheese.
15. Remove the enchiladas from the oven and let them cool for a few minutes.
16. Garnish with chopped fresh cilantro and sliced jalapeños (if using).
17. Serve hot with sour cream on the side, if desired.
18. Enjoy your delicious Chicken Enchiladas!

These Chicken Enchiladas are a crowd-pleasing Tex-Mex favorite that's perfect for a family dinner or gathering. You can customize the filling with your favorite vegetables and adjust the level of spiciness by adding more or less chili powder and diced jalapeños. Serve with a side of Mexican rice, refried beans, or a crisp green salad for a complete and satisfying meal. Enjoy the cheesy, flavorful goodness of these homemade enchiladas!

Pepperoni Pizza

Ingredients:

- 1 pound pizza dough (store-bought or homemade)
- 1/2 cup pizza sauce (store-bought or homemade)
- 2 cups shredded mozzarella cheese
- 1/2 cup sliced pepperoni
- Grated Parmesan cheese, for sprinkling
- Crushed red pepper flakes (optional)
- Fresh basil leaves, torn (optional)

Instructions:

1. Preheat your oven to the temperature specified on your pizza dough package or recipe (usually around 450°F or 230°C).
2. Roll out the pizza dough on a lightly floured surface into your desired shape (round, rectangular, etc.), about 12 inches in diameter for a standard pizza.
3. Transfer the rolled-out dough onto a pizza stone or a lightly greased baking sheet.
4. Spread the pizza sauce evenly over the dough, leaving a small border around the edges for the crust.
5. Sprinkle the shredded mozzarella cheese evenly over the sauce.
6. Arrange the sliced pepperoni on top of the cheese, covering the entire surface of the pizza.
7. Sprinkle grated Parmesan cheese over the pizza.
8. If desired, add a sprinkle of crushed red pepper flakes for extra heat.
9. Place the pizza in the preheated oven and bake for 12-15 minutes, or until the crust is golden brown and the cheese is bubbly and melted.
10. Remove the pizza from the oven and let it cool slightly.
11. Garnish with torn fresh basil leaves, if using.
12. Slice the pizza into wedges or squares and serve hot.

Enjoy your delicious homemade Pepperoni Pizza! This classic pizza is perfect for a casual dinner or a fun gathering with friends and family. Customize the toppings to your liking by adding additional vegetables, different types of cheese, or other meats. Serve with a side salad or garlic knots for a complete meal. Delight in the irresistible combination of gooey cheese, savory pepperoni, and flavorful sauce on a crispy pizza crust!

Corned Beef Hash

Ingredients:

- 2 tablespoons butter or vegetable oil
- 1 onion, finely chopped
- 2-3 cups cooked corned beef, diced (leftover or canned)
- 3-4 cups cooked potatoes, diced (leftover or boiled)
- Salt and pepper, to taste
- Optional: chopped fresh parsley or green onions for garnish
- Optional: fried eggs (to serve on top)

Instructions:

1. In a large skillet, melt the butter over medium heat.
2. Add the finely chopped onion to the skillet and sauté for 3-4 minutes until softened and translucent.
3. Add the diced corned beef to the skillet. Cook for 5-6 minutes, stirring occasionally, until the corned beef starts to brown slightly.
4. Add the diced cooked potatoes to the skillet with the corned beef and onions.
5. Season with salt and pepper to taste. Stir well to combine all ingredients.
6. Press down on the mixture with a spatula to compact it into the skillet.
7. Allow the hash to cook undisturbed for 5-7 minutes, or until the bottom is crispy and golden brown.
8. Use a spatula to flip sections of the hash to crisp up the other side. Cook for another 5-7 minutes until evenly browned and crispy.
9. Taste and adjust seasoning if needed.
10. Remove the skillet from heat and sprinkle with chopped fresh parsley or green onions for garnish.
11. Serve the corned beef hash hot, optionally topped with fried eggs.

This Corned Beef Hash is a hearty and comforting dish that's perfect for breakfast or brunch. It's a great way to use up leftover corned beef and potatoes from St. Patrick's Day or any occasion. Serve with a side of toast, English muffins, or biscuits. Enjoy the crispy, flavorful goodness of this classic hash dish!

Spinach and Feta Stuffed Chicken

Ingredients:

- 4 boneless, skinless chicken breasts
- Salt and pepper, to taste
- 1 tablespoon olive oil
- 2 cups fresh spinach leaves
- 1/2 cup crumbled feta cheese
- 2 cloves garlic, minced
- 1/4 teaspoon dried oregano
- 1/4 teaspoon dried basil
- 1/4 teaspoon dried thyme
- 1/4 teaspoon paprika
- Toothpicks or kitchen twine (for securing chicken)

Instructions:

1. Preheat the oven to 375°F (190°C).
2. Using a sharp knife, carefully butterfly each chicken breast by slicing horizontally along the side, but not all the way through, to create a pocket.
3. Season the inside of each chicken breast with salt and pepper.
4. In a skillet, heat the olive oil over medium heat.
5. Add minced garlic and sauté for 1 minute until fragrant.
6. Add fresh spinach to the skillet and cook until wilted, about 2-3 minutes.
7. Remove the skillet from heat and stir in crumbled feta cheese, dried oregano, dried basil, dried thyme, and paprika. Mix well until combined.
8. Stuff each chicken breast with the spinach and feta mixture, dividing it evenly among the chicken breasts. Use toothpicks or kitchen twine to secure the openings and keep the stuffing in place.
9. Heat a clean skillet over medium-high heat.
10. Sear the stuffed chicken breasts for 2-3 minutes on each side until golden brown.
11. Transfer the seared chicken breasts to a baking dish.
12. Bake in the preheated oven for 20-25 minutes, or until the chicken is cooked through and reaches an internal temperature of 165°F (74°C).
13. Remove the chicken from the oven and let it rest for a few minutes.
14. Carefully remove the toothpicks or kitchen twine before serving.
15. Slice the stuffed chicken breasts and serve hot.

Enjoy your delicious Spinach and Feta Stuffed Chicken! This recipe is a wonderful way to elevate plain chicken breasts with a flavorful and cheesy spinach filling. Serve with a side of roasted vegetables, rice, or a salad for a complete and satisfying meal. Your family and guests will love the combination of juicy chicken and savory spinach-feta stuffing!

Bacon, Lettuce, and Tomato Wrap

Ingredients:

- 4 large flour tortillas
- 8 slices cooked bacon
- 1 large tomato, thinly sliced
- 2 cups shredded lettuce (such as romaine or iceberg)
- Mayonnaise or ranch dressing
- Salt and pepper, to taste

Instructions:

1. Lay out the flour tortillas on a clean surface.
2. Spread a thin layer of mayonnaise or ranch dressing over each tortilla.
3. Arrange the shredded lettuce evenly down the center of each tortilla.
4. Place 2 slices of cooked bacon on top of the lettuce on each tortilla.
5. Top the bacon with thinly sliced tomatoes.
6. Season the tomatoes with salt and pepper, to taste.
7. Fold in the sides of each tortilla, then roll up tightly to form wraps.
8. Cut each wrap in half diagonally, if desired, for easier handling.
9. Serve immediately and enjoy your delicious Bacon, Lettuce, and Tomato Wraps!

These BLT wraps are a quick and satisfying meal, perfect for lunch or a light dinner. Customize the wraps by adding sliced avocado, grilled chicken, or cheese for extra flavor and texture. Pair with potato chips, pickles, or a side salad for a complete meal. Enjoy the classic combination of crispy bacon, juicy tomatoes, and crunchy lettuce wrapped in a soft tortilla!

Teriyaki Beef Bowl

Ingredients:

- 1 lb beef sirloin or flank steak, thinly sliced
- 1 tablespoon vegetable oil
- 1/2 cup teriyaki sauce (store-bought or homemade)
- 2 cups cooked white or brown rice
- 1 cup broccoli florets
- 1 bell pepper, sliced
- 1 carrot, sliced
- Sesame seeds, for garnish (optional)
- Sliced green onions, for garnish (optional)

Instructions:

1. Heat vegetable oil in a large skillet or wok over medium-high heat.
2. Add the thinly sliced beef to the skillet and cook for 2-3 minutes until browned.
3. Pour teriyaki sauce over the beef in the skillet. Stir well to coat the beef in the sauce.
4. Add broccoli florets, sliced bell pepper, and sliced carrot to the skillet. Stir-fry for an additional 3-4 minutes until the vegetables are tender-crisp and the beef is cooked to your liking.
5. Reduce heat to low and simmer for 1-2 minutes to allow the flavors to meld.
6. Serve the teriyaki beef and vegetables over cooked rice in bowls.
7. Garnish with sesame seeds and sliced green onions, if desired.
8. Enjoy your delicious Teriyaki Beef Bowl!

This Teriyaki Beef Bowl is a tasty and satisfying dish that's quick and easy to make. The tender slices of beef cooked in a savory teriyaki sauce with colorful vegetables served over rice make a perfect meal for lunch or dinner. Feel free to customize the vegetables based on your preference, and add extra teriyaki sauce or soy sauce for more flavor. Enjoy this flavorful Japanese-inspired dish with your favorite garnishes!

Chicken Fajitas

Ingredients:

- 1 lb chicken breast, thinly sliced
- 1 onion, sliced
- 1 bell pepper (any color), sliced
- 2 tablespoons vegetable oil
- 2 tablespoons fajita seasoning (store-bought or homemade)
- Salt and pepper, to taste
- Flour tortillas, for serving
- Optional toppings: shredded cheese, sour cream, salsa, guacamole, chopped cilantro, lime wedges

Instructions:

1. In a bowl, combine the sliced chicken breast with the fajita seasoning, salt, and pepper. Toss to coat the chicken evenly.
2. Heat vegetable oil in a large skillet or cast-iron pan over medium-high heat.
3. Add the seasoned chicken to the skillet and cook for 5-6 minutes, stirring occasionally, until the chicken is browned and cooked through.
4. Remove the cooked chicken from the skillet and set aside.
5. In the same skillet, add the sliced onion and bell pepper. Cook for 4-5 minutes, stirring occasionally, until the vegetables are tender-crisp and slightly charred.
6. Return the cooked chicken to the skillet with the vegetables. Stir to combine and heat everything together for another minute or two.
7. Warm the flour tortillas in a dry skillet or microwave.
8. Spoon the chicken and vegetable mixture onto the warmed tortillas.
9. Serve the chicken fajitas with optional toppings such as shredded cheese, sour cream, salsa, guacamole, chopped cilantro, and lime wedges.
10. Roll up the tortillas and enjoy your delicious Chicken Fajitas!

These Chicken Fajitas are a flavorful Tex-Mex favorite that's perfect for a quick and satisfying meal. Customize the fajitas with your favorite toppings and serve with rice, beans, or a side salad for a complete dinner. Enjoy the tender chicken and colorful vegetables wrapped in warm tortillas, bursting with delicious Mexican flavors!

Italian Sub Sandwich

Ingredients:

- Italian sub rolls or hoagie rolls
- 4-6 slices each of deli meats (such as salami, pepperoni, ham, and/or prosciutto)
- 4-6 slices of provolone cheese
- Sliced tomatoes
- Sliced red onions
- Sliced pepperoncini peppers (optional)
- Shredded lettuce
- Olive oil
- Red wine vinegar
- Salt and pepper, to taste
- Italian seasoning (optional)
- Mayonnaise or mustard (optional)

Instructions:

1. Preheat the oven to 350°F (175°C) to toast the sub rolls, if desired.
2. Slice the Italian sub rolls or hoagie rolls horizontally, but do not cut all the way through.
3. Layer the deli meats and provolone cheese inside the rolls.
4. Add sliced tomatoes, red onions, and pepperoncini peppers on top of the cheese.
5. Sprinkle shredded lettuce over the vegetables.
6. Drizzle olive oil and red wine vinegar over the sandwich filling.
7. Season with salt, pepper, and Italian seasoning, if desired.
8. Optionally, spread mayonnaise or mustard on the inside of the top half of the roll.
9. Close the sandwiches and wrap each one tightly in aluminum foil.
10. Place the foil-wrapped sandwiches on a baking sheet and bake in the preheated oven for 10-15 minutes, or until the bread is toasted and the cheese is melted.
11. Remove the sandwiches from the oven and let them cool slightly.
12. Unwrap the foil from the sandwiches.
13. Slice the Italian sub sandwiches in half or into smaller portions.
14. Serve hot and enjoy your delicious Italian Sub Sandwiches!

These Italian Sub Sandwiches are loaded with savory deli meats, cheese, and fresh vegetables, making them a satisfying and flavorful meal. Customize the sandwiches with your favorite Italian meats, cheeses, and toppings. Serve with potato chips, pickles, or a side salad for a complete lunch or dinner. Enjoy the classic combination of flavors in this delicious and hearty sub sandwich!

Veggie and Hummus Wrap

Ingredients:

- Large whole wheat or spinach tortillas
- Hummus (store-bought or homemade)
- Assorted sliced vegetables (such as bell peppers, cucumber, carrots, red onion, lettuce, and tomatoes)
- Optional additions: avocado slices, sprouts, shredded cabbage
- Salt and pepper, to taste

Instructions:

1. Lay out a large tortilla on a clean surface.
2. Spread a generous layer of hummus evenly over the tortilla, leaving a small border around the edges.
3. Arrange sliced vegetables over the hummus in a single layer, covering the tortilla evenly.
4. Season the vegetables with salt and pepper, if desired.
5. Add optional additions like avocado slices, sprouts, or shredded cabbage for extra flavor and texture.
6. Starting from one end, tightly roll up the tortilla to enclose the filling.
7. Slice the wrap in half diagonally, if desired, for easier handling.
8. Serve immediately and enjoy your delicious Veggie and Hummus Wrap!

This Veggie and Hummus Wrap is a healthy and satisfying meal option that's perfect for lunch or a quick dinner. Feel free to customize the wrap with your favorite vegetables and add-ons. It's a great way to pack in nutritious ingredients and enjoy a flavorful and portable meal on the go. Serve with a side of fresh fruit or a small salad for a complete and balanced meal. Enjoy the crunchy, creamy, and delicious combination of flavors in this veggie-packed wrap!

Beef Stroganoff

Ingredients:

- 1 lb beef sirloin or tenderloin, thinly sliced
- Salt and pepper, to taste
- 2 tablespoons olive oil
- 1 onion, finely chopped
- 2 cloves garlic, minced
- 8 oz mushrooms, sliced
- 2 tablespoons all-purpose flour
- 1 cup beef broth
- 1 tablespoon Dijon mustard
- 2 tablespoons Worcestershire sauce
- 1 cup sour cream
- Cooked egg noodles or rice, for serving
- Chopped fresh parsley, for garnish (optional)

Instructions:

1. Season the thinly sliced beef with salt and pepper.
2. In a large skillet or frying pan, heat the olive oil over medium-high heat.
3. Add the seasoned beef to the skillet and cook for 2-3 minutes until browned. Remove the beef from the skillet and set aside.
4. In the same skillet, add the chopped onion and cook for 2-3 minutes until softened.
5. Add the minced garlic and sliced mushrooms to the skillet. Cook for another 4-5 minutes until the mushrooms are golden brown and cooked through.
6. Sprinkle the flour over the mushrooms and onions. Stir well to combine and cook for 1 minute.
7. Gradually pour in the beef broth, stirring constantly to prevent lumps.
8. Stir in the Dijon mustard and Worcestershire sauce. Bring the mixture to a simmer and cook for 2-3 minutes until slightly thickened.
9. Reduce heat to low. Stir in the sour cream until well combined and heated through.
10. Return the cooked beef to the skillet and stir to coat it with the sauce.
11. Cook for another 2-3 minutes, stirring occasionally, until the beef is heated through.
12. Taste and adjust seasoning with salt and pepper, if needed.

13. Serve the beef stroganoff over cooked egg noodles or rice.
14. Garnish with chopped fresh parsley, if desired.
15. Enjoy your delicious Beef Stroganoff!

This Beef Stroganoff recipe is creamy, flavorful, and comforting. Serve it over cooked egg noodles or rice for a satisfying meal that's perfect for family dinners or special occasions. Garnish with fresh parsley for a pop of color and freshness. Enjoy the tender beef and savory mushroom sauce in this classic Russian-inspired dish!

Baked Lemon Herb Cod

Ingredients:

- 4 cod fillets (about 6 oz each), skinless and boneless
- 2 tablespoons olive oil
- 2 tablespoons fresh lemon juice
- Zest of 1 lemon
- 2 cloves garlic, minced
- 1 teaspoon dried thyme
- 1 teaspoon dried parsley
- Salt and pepper, to taste
- Lemon slices, for garnish
- Chopped fresh parsley, for garnish

Instructions:

1. Preheat your oven to 400°F (200°C). Lightly grease a baking dish with olive oil or non-stick cooking spray.
2. Place the cod fillets in the prepared baking dish in a single layer.
3. In a small bowl, whisk together the olive oil, lemon juice, lemon zest, minced garlic, dried thyme, dried parsley, salt, and pepper.
4. Pour the lemon herb mixture evenly over the cod fillets, coating them well.
5. Place a few lemon slices on top of each fillet for extra flavor and presentation.
6. Bake the cod in the preheated oven for 12-15 minutes, or until the fish is opaque and flakes easily with a fork.
7. Remove the baked cod from the oven and let it rest for a few minutes.
8. Garnish with chopped fresh parsley before serving.
9. Serve the baked lemon herb cod with your favorite side dishes, such as steamed vegetables, rice, or a salad.
10. Enjoy your delicious and flavorful Baked Lemon Herb Cod!

This Baked Lemon Herb Cod recipe is simple, healthy, and bursting with fresh flavors. The combination of lemon, garlic, and herbs enhances the delicate flavor of the cod. Serve this dish for a light and satisfying meal that's perfect for any occasion. Enjoy the tender and flaky cod with a bright and zesty lemon herb sauce!

Pulled Pork Sliders

Ingredients:

- 2 lbs pork shoulder or pork butt
- Salt and pepper, to taste
- 1 tablespoon vegetable oil
- 1 onion, finely chopped
- 4 cloves garlic, minced
- 1 cup barbecue sauce (store-bought or homemade)
- Slider buns or small dinner rolls
- Coleslaw (optional, for topping)

Instructions:

1. Season the pork shoulder or pork butt with salt and pepper.
2. In a large skillet or Dutch oven, heat the vegetable oil over medium-high heat.
3. Sear the seasoned pork on all sides until browned, about 3-4 minutes per side.
4. Transfer the seared pork to a slow cooker.
5. Add chopped onion and minced garlic to the skillet. Cook for 2-3 minutes until softened.
6. Pour the cooked onion and garlic over the pork in the slow cooker.
7. Pour barbecue sauce over the pork.
8. Cover and cook on low heat for 8-10 hours or on high heat for 4-5 hours, until the pork is tender and falls apart easily.
9. Once cooked, shred the pork using two forks to pull it apart.
10. Toast the slider buns or dinner rolls in the oven or a toaster oven until lightly browned.
11. Fill each bun or roll with a generous portion of pulled pork.
12. Top with coleslaw, if desired, for added crunch and freshness.
13. Serve immediately and enjoy your delicious Pulled Pork Sliders!

These Pulled Pork Sliders are perfect for parties, gatherings, or casual meals. The tender and flavorful pulled pork pairs perfectly with soft slider buns and tangy barbecue sauce. Add coleslaw on top for a refreshing contrast in texture. Serve with pickles, potato chips, or fries for a complete and satisfying meal. Enjoy these mouthwatering sliders with family and friends!

Thai Peanut Noodles

Ingredients:

- 8 oz (225g) rice noodles (or any noodles of your choice)
- 1/2 cup creamy peanut butter
- 1/4 cup soy sauce (or tamari for gluten-free)
- 3 tablespoons rice vinegar
- 2 tablespoons honey (or maple syrup for vegan option)
- 1 tablespoon sesame oil
- 2 cloves garlic, minced
- 1 tablespoon finely grated fresh ginger
- 1/4 teaspoon red pepper flakes (adjust to taste)
- Juice of 1 lime
- 1/4 cup warm water (to thin the sauce)
- Optional toppings: chopped green onions, chopped cilantro, chopped peanuts, sliced red bell pepper, shredded carrots

Instructions:

1. Cook the Noodles:
    - Cook the rice noodles according to the package instructions. Once cooked, drain and rinse the noodles under cold water to stop them from cooking further. Set aside.
2. Make the Peanut Sauce:
    - In a medium bowl, whisk together peanut butter, soy sauce, rice vinegar, honey, sesame oil, minced garlic, grated ginger, red pepper flakes, and lime juice until smooth.
    - Add warm water gradually to the sauce, whisking continuously until you achieve a smooth and creamy consistency. Adjust the amount of water based on how thick or thin you prefer the sauce.
3. Combine the Noodles and Sauce:
    - Place the cooked and rinsed noodles in a large mixing bowl.
    - Pour the peanut sauce over the noodles and toss well to coat the noodles evenly with the sauce.
4. Serve:
    - Divide the Thai peanut noodles into serving bowls.
    - Garnish with chopped green onions, cilantro, chopped peanuts, sliced red bell pepper, and shredded carrots, if desired.
5. Enjoy:

- Serve the Thai peanut noodles immediately and enjoy the delicious flavors!

Tips:

- For added protein, toss in cooked chicken, shrimp, tofu, or edamame.
- Adjust the sweetness and saltiness of the sauce to your taste by adding more honey or soy sauce as needed.
- If you prefer a spicier sauce, increase the amount of red pepper flakes or add a dash of sriracha sauce.
- These noodles can be enjoyed warm or cold, making them a versatile dish for any occasion.

By following these steps, you'll have a flavorful and satisfying plate of Thai Peanut Noodles ready to enjoy!

www.ingramcontent.com/pod-product-compliance
Lightning Source LLC
LaVergne TN
LVHW081613060526
838201LV00054B/2233